A Kid's Book of Experiments With

LIGHT

Robert Gardner
and
Joshua Conklin

SURPRISING Science Experiments

Enslow Publishing
101 W. 23rd Street
Suite 240
New York, NY 10011
USA

enslow.com

Published in 2016 by Enslow Publishing, LLC
101 W. 23rd Street, Suite 240, New York, NY 10011

Library of Congress Cataloging-in-Publication Data

Gardner, Robert, 1929- author.
 A kid's book of experiments with light / Robert Gardner and Joshua Conklin.
    pages cm. — (Surprising science experiments)
  Includes bibliographical references and index.
 ISBN 978-0-7660-7205-3 (library binding)
 ISBN 978-0-7660-7203-9 (pbk.)
 ISBN 978-0-7660-7204-6 (6-pack)
1. Light—Experiments—Juvenile literature. 2. Science—Experiments—Juvenile literature. 3. Science projects—Juvenile literature. I. Conklin, Joshua, author. II. Title.
 QC365.G37 2016
 535.078—dc23
                                     2015029982

Printed in the United States of America

To Our Readers: We have done our best to make sure all website addresses in this book were active and appropriate when we went to press. However, the author and the publisher have no control over and assume no liability for the material available on those websites or on any websites they may link to. Any comments or suggestions can be sent by e-mail to customerservice@enslow.com.

Photo Credits: Throughout book: Wiktoria Pawlak/Shutterstock.com (lightbulbs), VLADGRIN/Shutterstock.com (science background), Aleksandrs Bondars/Shutterstock.com (colorful banners), vector-RGB/Shutterstock.com (arrows); cover, p. 1 Sapann-Design/Shutterstock.com (colorful alphabet); Login/Shutterstock.com (rainbow wheel); Funny Solution Studio/Shutterstock.com (kid with magnifying glass); p. 4 Yuganov Konstantin/Shutterstock.com; p. 12 donatas1205/Shutterstock.com; p. 33 Aaron Amat/Shutterstock.com; p. 36 Loskutinikov/Shutterstock.com; p. 41 Shubham Dhingra/EyeEm/Getty Images; p. 45 RickMcEvoy/Loop Images/SuperStock.

Illustration Credits: Accurate Art, Inc. c/o George Barile.

CONTENTS

Introduction

Unless you live under a large opaque object (more on what *opaque* means later) like a rock, you spend most of your day in the light. When you wake up and rub the dreams from your eyes, light is there to greet you. If you need a drink of water in the middle of the night, you will not get very far without a night-light or at least a little moonlight. In this book we will learn about light by conducting experiments. By the end of the book you will know a lot more about how light behaves. Let's get to work!

Light's Path

Light does not have feet and can't take a walk down the street. However, light does follow a path from its original source. Some examples of an original source include the sun or a light bulb. So, what kind of path does light follow? Let's do some experiments to find out.

Experiment 1: How Light Travels

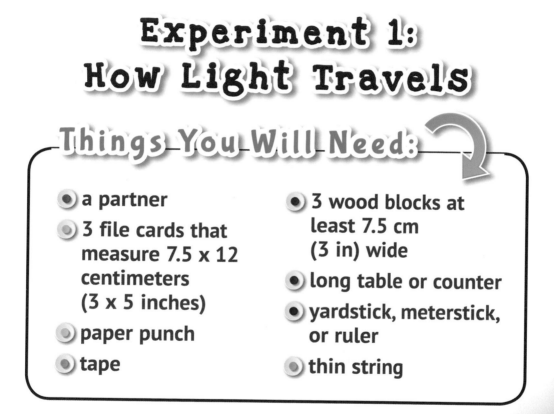

Things You Will Need:

- a partner
- 3 file cards that measure 7.5 x 12 centimeters (3 x 5 inches)
- paper punch
- tape
- 3 wood blocks at least 7.5 cm (3 in) wide
- long table or counter
- yardstick, meterstick, or ruler
- thin string

1. Hold together three file cards that measure 7.5 x 12 cm (3 x 5 in). They should look like a single card (Figure 1a). Use a paper punch to make holes in the same spot on all three cards at the same time.

2. Tape each card to one of three identical wood blocks. The bottom edges of the cards should touch the bottom edges of the blocks (Figure 1b).

3. Put the blocks about 50 cm (20 in) apart on a long table or counter near a window.

4. Look through the hole farthest from the window. You will see light from outside coming through the hole. Move the second block until you see light coming through both holes.

5. Ask a partner to slowly move the third block until you see light coming through all three holes.

6. Cut a piece of thin string about two meters (yards) long. Have your partner hold one end of the string while you hold the other end. Carefully thread the string through all three holes without moving the cards. Gently tighten the string. Do the holes lie along a straight line? What does this tell you about the path followed by light?

Figure 1

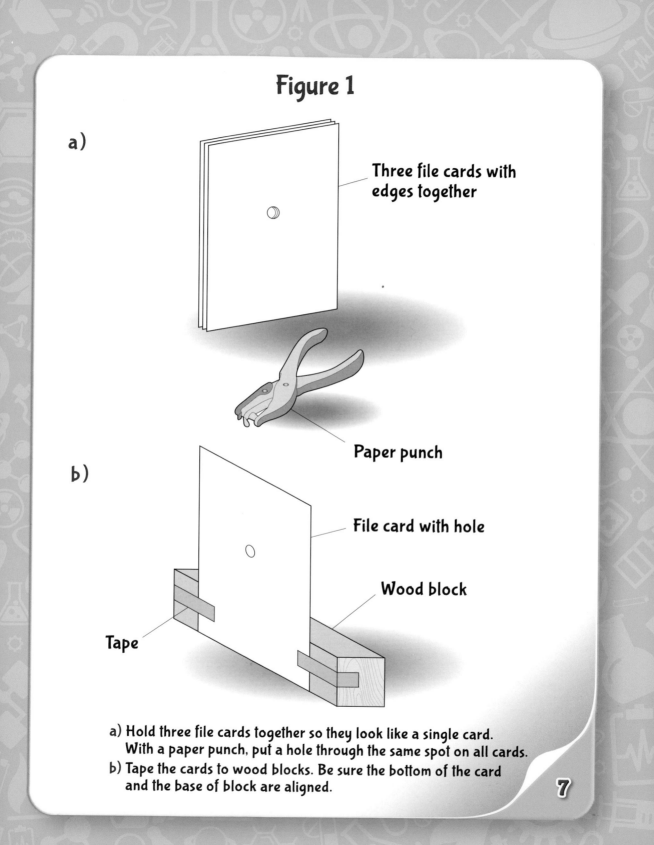

a) **Three file cards with edges together**

Paper punch

b) **File card with hole**

Wood block

Tape

a) Hold three file cards together so they look like a single card. With a paper punch, put a hole through the same spot on all cards.

b) Tape the cards to wood blocks. Be sure the bottom of the card and the base of block are aligned.

Experiment 2: Light's Path Through a Pinhole

Things You Will Need:

- an adult
- a room that is dark with a light-colored wall
- clear light bulb such as a tubular showcase bulb with one long vertical filament
- table
- lamp
- thick pin or small nail
- large sheet of cardboard

1. Find a room you can make dark.

2. **Ask an adult** to put a clear light bulb (one in which the filament can be seen, such as a clear tubular bulb) into a lamp socket on a table. The lamp should be about 60 cm (2 ft) from a light-colored wall.

3. Use a thick pin or small nail to make a hole in the center of a large sheet of cardboard.

4. Make the room dark.

5. Place the cardboard sheet with the pinhole between the clear light bulb and the light-colored wall (Figure 2.) Light coming through the pinhole will strike the wall.

Notice the image of the light bulb on the wall. Is it right side up or upside down?

6. To find out, move a pencil up and down in front of the light bulb. What do you find?

7. Move the pinhole closer to the wall. What happens to the image? What happens to the image if you move the pinhole farther from the wall?

How does this experiment show that light travels in straight lines?

Light's Path: An Explanation

You discovered light walks a straight path! The string and the narrow light beam traveled a straight line through the three holes. This is true as long as light remains in a single substance such as air. We will see what happens when light travels through a different substance later.

Since light travels in straight lines, it can make images when it passes through a small opening. The shadow of the pencil went in the opposite direction on the image when you moved it up and down, proving the image was upside down.

Figure 2 shows how a ray of light ends up flipped when traveling from the bulb to the image on the wall. The ray at the top of the light ends up at the bottom of the image.

Figure 2

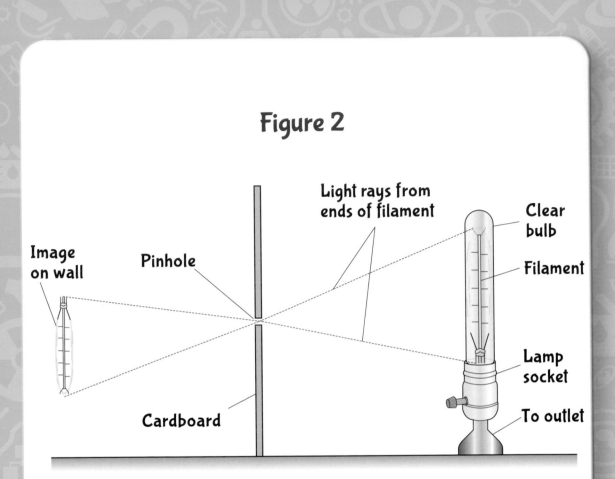

Light rays from ends of filament

Clear bulb

Filament

Image on wall

Pinhole

Lamp socket

Cardboard

To outlet

Light from the clear bulb's filament will produce an image after passing through a pinhole.

You can also make your own drawing of Figure 2. Then draw straight lines from various spots on the bulb to the image to discover where the lines end up on corresponding parts of the upside-down image. Only straight lines (rays) of light can explain a pinhole image.

IDEAS
for a
Science Project

- Design an experiment to show light traveling in straight lines in water.

- Build a pinhole camera and take photographs. Why will you need long exposure times?

- How can you explain the pinhole images of the sun (sun dapples) that you can see in the shade of a leafy tree on a sunny day?

- Move your eyes so close to the print on this page that the print becomes blurry. Then hold an index card with a pinhole in front of your eye. Why can you now read the print?

This photo was taken with a pinhole camera.

Transparent, Translucent, or Opaque

When you wake up in the morning and the sun is shining, it feels like light is everywhere. It streams through your windows, shimmers through your curtains, and bounces off your dresser. While light goes anywhere it is allowed to shine, it reacts differently when it reaches various objects. Let's explore below.

Opaque Objects

Opaque objects, like your dresser, reflect light back to your eyes. They may also absorb some light. The more light they absorb, the dimmer they appear. No light can come through opaque objects, such as thick wood or metal.

Transparent Objects

Things that are transparent, such as windows, allow light to pass right through them. It's almost as if they are not there.

Translucent Objects

Things that are translucent, like a thin curtain, allow some light to pass through them, but they scatter or absorb some of the light, too.

Experiment 3: Which Things Are Transparent, Translucent, or Opaque?

Things You Will Need:

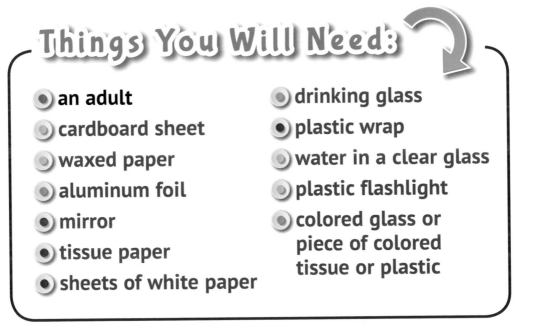

- an adult
- cardboard sheet
- waxed paper
- aluminum foil
- mirror
- tissue paper
- sheets of white paper
- drinking glass
- plastic wrap
- water in a clear glass
- plastic flashlight
- colored glass or piece of colored tissue or plastic

1. Gather as many of the items listed as you can but also feel free to grab some other objects as well. To test the items you have gathered, hold each one in front of a bright window or a light bulb.

2. Decide whether each object is transparent, translucent, or opaque. You probably found that one sheet of white paper is translucent. What about a stack of white paper?

Figure 3

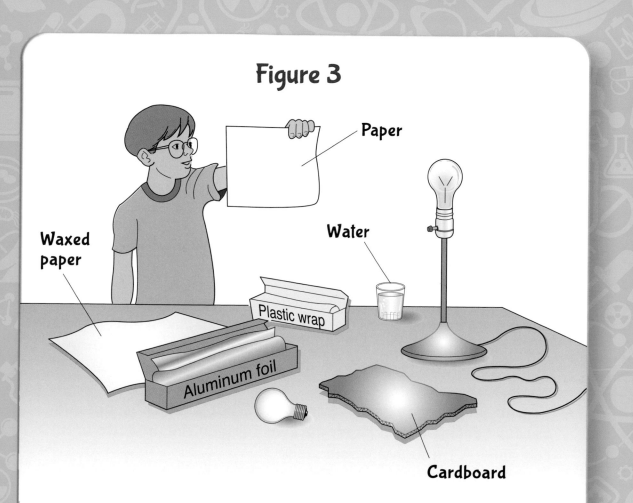

Paper

Water

Waxed paper

Plastic wrap

Aluminum foil

Cardboard

3. Hold a piece of colored glass or a piece of colored tissue or plastic in front of a light source. How would you classify the colored material?

4. What about your body?

Close your eyes in front of a bright window. Are your eyelids opaque or translucent? To help you decide, cover your closed eyes with your hands. What do you conclude?

In a very dark room and with **an adult** present, take a plastic flashlight, gently place the lighted tip in your mouth, and close your lips. Are your cheeks opaque or translucent? (You may need the adult to tell you. Have the adult do it too!)

Transparent, Translucent, or Opaque: An Explanation

The transparent objects likely included glass, water, and plastic wrap. Translucent items included waxed paper, white paper, tissue paper, your eyelids, and your cheeks. Cardboard, aluminum foil, a mirror, your hand, and a stack of white paper are all opaque objects.

One sheet of paper is translucent, but a stack is opaque because each sheet of paper absorbs some of the light. No light can make it through a whole stack.

Water creates a similar effect. Much of the light that strikes water is reflected. So even though water is clear it appears blue when seen beneath a bright blue sky. Some of the light that strikes water is absorbed. This is why an ocean diver will be surrounded by less and less light as he descends.

Later we will learn that ordinary light, sometimes called white light, is actually many colors! Items like the colored glass, tissue, or plastic allowed only light of the same color to pass through (Figure 4). Light of other colors was mostly absorbed.

Figure 4

Green glass

Light, Opaque Objects, and Shadows

This book is opaque. When light strikes an opaque object it is absorbed, reflected, or both. This makes it darker on the side opposite the light source. We call this darker area a shadow. If you are reading this book in a room with an overhead light you can pick the book up and see a shadow on the surface below.

You have probably spent time observing or even dancing with your shadow on a sunny day. Your shadow lengthens and shortens based on the position of the sun. Your shadow grows shorter in the morning, is shortest at midday (noon), and lengthens again as the sun sets.

On a bright sunny day, check your shadow every hour. When is your shadow longest? When is it shortest? Why do you think the length of your shadow changes?

Experiment 4: Shadows Sharp and Fuzzy

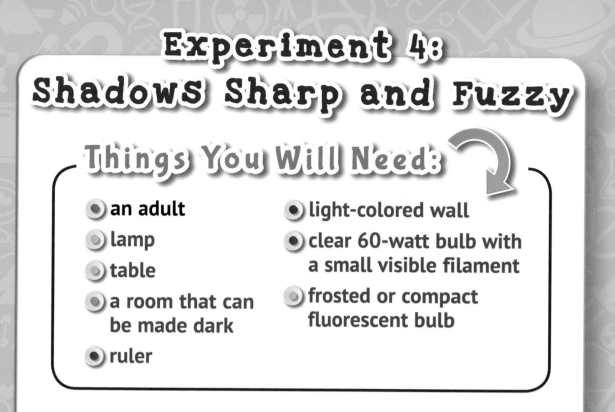

Things You Will Need:

- an adult
- lamp
- table
- a room that can be made dark
- ruler
- light-colored wall
- clear 60-watt bulb with a small visible filament
- frosted or compact fluorescent bulb

1. Place a lamp on a table in a dark room about 60 cm (2 feet) from a light-colored wall.

2. **Ask an adult** to screw a clear 60-watt bulb with a small visible filament (Figure 5a) into the lamp socket. Light from this bulb comes from a very small area.

3. Turn on the light. Hold your hand halfway between the bulb and the wall. Notice that your hand's shadow is quite sharp. Does it become sharper if you move your hand closer to the wall?

4. Next, **ask an adult** to remove the clear bulb and replace it with a frosted or compact fluorescent bulb (Figure 5b). Light from this bulb comes from a larger area.

5. Again, hold your hand about halfway between the bulb and the wall. Notice that the shadow is fuzzy. Does it become sharper if you move your hand closer to the wall?

6. Why do you think the shadows are different when you use different bulbs? It may help if you think about what you learned in Experiment 2.

Figure 5

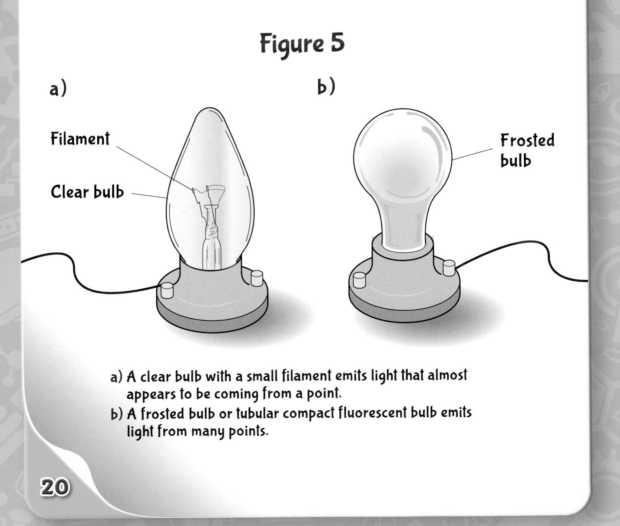

a)

Filament

Clear bulb

b)

Frosted bulb

a) A clear bulb with a small filament emits light that almost appears to be coming from a point.
b) A frosted bulb or tubular compact fluorescent bulb emits light from many points.

Shadows Sharp and Fuzzy: An Explanation

A point of light (clear bulb) acts like light that has gone through a pinhole. It creates sharp shadows (Figure 6a) because no other light can reach the shadow.

Light from many points (a frosted bulb or the sun on a larger scale) allows some light to fall on parts of the shadow. That makes the shadow fuzzy (Figure 6b).

Late on a sunny afternoon look at your shadow. The part near your feet is dark (umbra). The more distant part, the shadow of your head, is fuzzy (penumbra). So every sunny afternoon you have a fuzzy head!

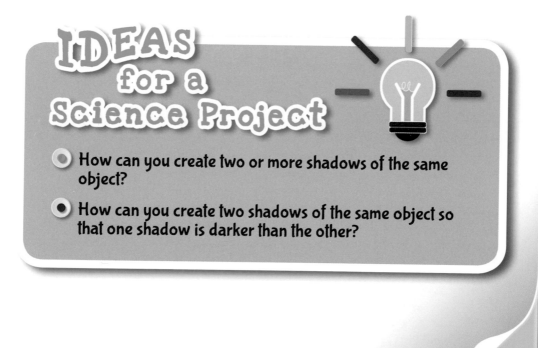

IDEAS for a Science Project

- How can you create two or more shadows of the same object?

- How can you create two shadows of the same object so that one shadow is darker than the other?

Figure 6

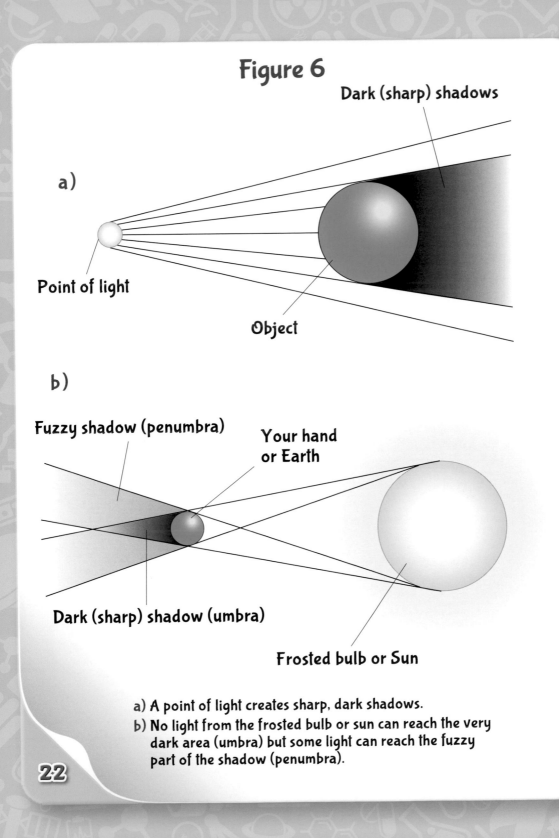

a)

Dark (sharp) shadows

Point of light

Object

b)

Fuzzy shadow (penumbra)

Your hand
or Earth

Dark (sharp) shadow (umbra)

Frosted bulb or Sun

a) A point of light creates sharp, dark shadows.
b) No light from the frosted bulb or sun can reach the very
   dark area (umbra) but some light can reach the fuzzy
   part of the shadow (penumbra).

Light Can Be Reflected

Take a look in a mirror … you are looking good! Did you know that your image is actually light being reflected from the mirror? The light is not absorbed or transmitted like with a transparent or translucent object but reflected back into your eyes. Let's learn more about how it works.

Experiment 5: Where IS Your Mirror Image?

Things You Will Need:

- a partner
- a mirror such as one on a wall
- small mirror about 5 x 8 cm (2 x 3 in)
- ruler
- small pencil (about as tall as the small mirror)
- clay
- long pencil

1. Look into a mirror. Where does your image appear to be located? Many people think the image is on the mirror's surface. Is that where it appears?

2. Have someone stand behind you while you look into a mirror. Does that person's image appear to be on top of yours or behind yours?

3. You can locate a mirror image. Suppose two things are at the same place. They will stay together when you move your head from side to side or when you close one eye and then the other (wink). If they are not in the same place, the one closer to you will appear to move relative to the other.

   See how it works! Hold one finger in front of you at arm's length. Hold the other finger close to your face. Now look at both fingers. Look first with your right eye, then with your left. You can either turn your head from side to side or wink one eye and then the other (if you need help winking ask your partner to gently close one eye at a time for you). You'll see the nearer finger shift (move) relative to the distant finger.

   Now hold one finger on top of the other at arm's length. Again, close one eye and then the other or turn your head from side to side. This time the fingers stay together. They do not shift because they are at the same place.

4. Place a short pencil about 10 cm (4 in) in front of a small mirror (Figure 7). The pencil should be about as tall as the mirror. Use lumps of clay to support the objects.

5. Hold a second taller pencil behind the mirror. Put your head behind the short pencil in front of the mirror. You can see the image of the short pencil in the mirror. And you can see the top of the second taller pencil behind the mirror.

6. Move the taller pencil back and forth (not side to side) behind the mirror to different positions. Keep it in line with the image of the pencil in front of the mirror. At each position, look first with your right eye and then with your left. Keep moving the pencil slowly and winking your eyes. Do this until the mirror image and the tall pencil "stick" together. Now you know the tall pencil is at the same place as the image of the short pencil.

7. Measure the distance from the mirror to the pencil in front of the mirror. Then measure the distance from the mirror to the pencil behind the mirror (the position of the image). How do these distances compare?

Figure 7

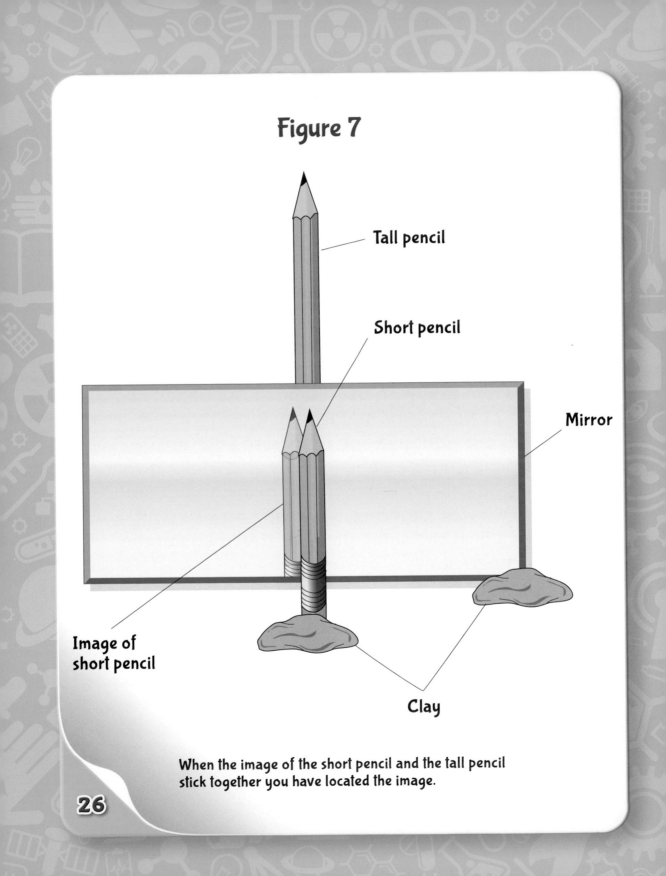

Tall pencil

Short pencil

Mirror

Image of
short pencil

Clay

When the image of the short pencil and the tall pencil
stick together you have located the image.

Experiment 6: How Is Light Reflected?

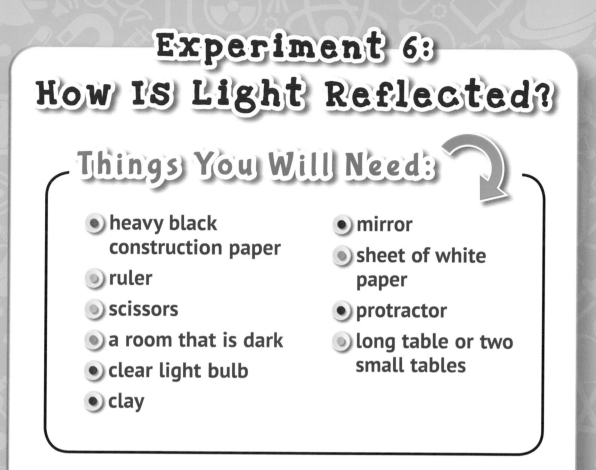

Things You Will Need:

- heavy black construction paper
- ruler
- scissors
- a room that is dark
- clear light bulb
- clay
- mirror
- sheet of white paper
- protractor
- long table or two small tables

Let's try another experiment to learn more about how light is reflected.

1. Find a sheet of heavy black construction paper and cut a rectangle that is about 10 cm (4 in) x 15 cm (6 in).

2 Find the center of one long side of the rectangle and carefully cut a narrow (1 mm wide) vertical slit . Make the slit about 6 cm (2.5 in) long.

3. Fold about 3 cm (1.5 in) of the paper at each end so it will stand upright (Figure 8a).

4. In a room that can be made dark, set up the experiment as shown in Figure 8b. Use either of the clear light bulbs you used in Experiments 2 or 4. The light bulb should be about one meter (100 cm) or yard from the black upright paper. Stick a piece of clay to the back bottom of the mirror. This will keep the mirror upright on a sheet of white paper.

5. Make the room dark and turn on the clear bulb.

6. The narrow beam (ray) of light will reflect from the mirror. Turn the mirror to change the angle at which the light ray hits the mirror.

The ray coming from the light to the mirror is called the incident ray. The ray reflected by the mirror is called—you guessed it—the reflected ray. Use a protractor to measure the angle between the incident ray and the mirror (angle i). Use the same protractor to measure the angle between the reflected ray and the mirror (angle r). Be sure the center of the protractor's base is at the point where reflection takes place. Have **an adult** help if needed.

How do the two angles (i and r) compare?

Figure 8

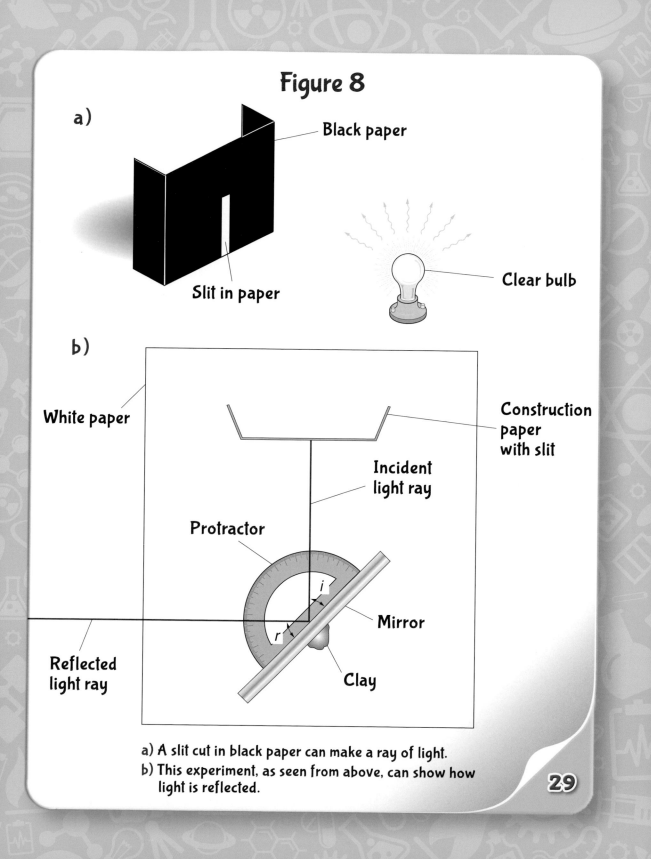

a)

Black paper

Slit in paper

Clear bulb

b)

White paper

Construction paper with slit

Incident light ray

Protractor

i

r

Mirror

Reflected light ray

Clay

a) A slit cut in black paper can make a ray of light.
b) This experiment, as seen from above, can show how light is reflected.

7. Turn the mirror to change the angle between the incident ray and the mirror. Measure angle *r* for many different values of angle *i*. How do the two angles compare?

You may have found a scientific law—something that is always true! How would you state your law? What would you call it?

Light Can Be Reflected: An Explanation

Although mirror images appear to be behind the mirror, many people do not believe it. You, however, *proved* that the images really exist. Of course, if you actually peeked behind a mirror you would not see an image. The reason is that the image created by a mirror is a virtual image, one that seems to be in a certain place because of the way light rays from the object are reflected. Figure 9 shows how a virtual image is formed.

You hopefully found that angles *i* and *r* were always equal (or nearly equal) no matter how you rotated the mirror. This is the "law of reflection". When light is reflected, the angle of incidence equals the angle of reflection. Congratulations on proving a scientific law!

Figure 9

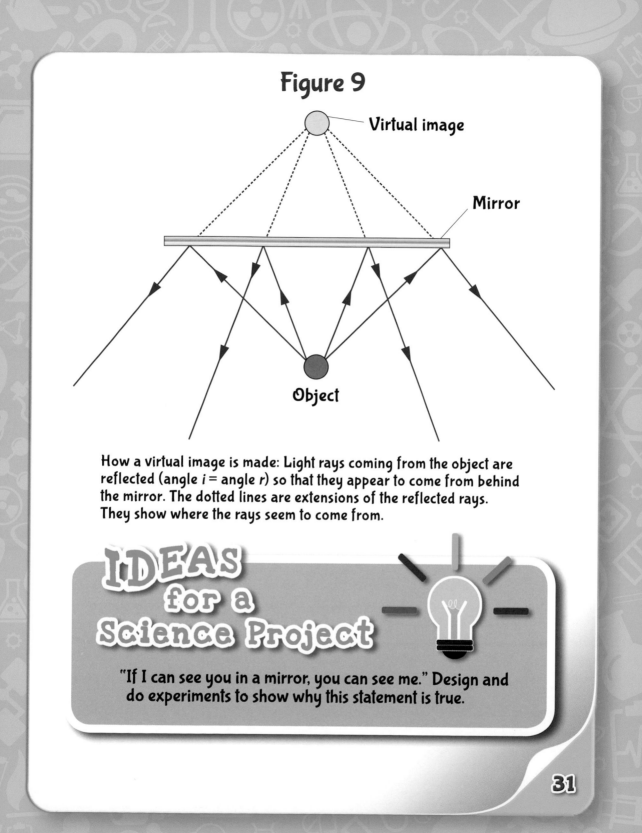

How a virtual image is made: Light rays coming from the object are reflected (angle *i* = angle *r*) so that they appear to come from behind the mirror. The dotted lines are extensions of the reflected rays. They show where the rays seem to come from.

IDEAS for a Science Project

"If I can see you in a mirror, you can see me." Design and do experiments to show why this statement is true.

Bending Light With Water and Glass (Refraction)

We have previously seen light traveling in a straight path. Does it ever turn or bend? Moving straight ahead must get boring eventually.

Light travels in straight lines within air, water, glass, or any transparent substance. But what happens when it passes from one substance to another? Let's find out!

Experiment 7: Strange Things To See

Things You Will Need:

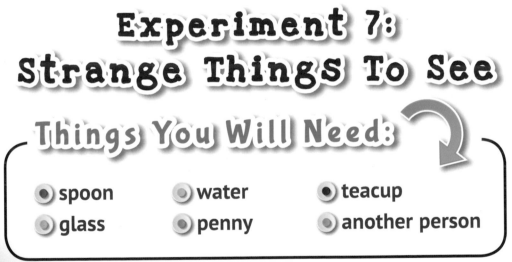

- spoon
- glass
- water
- penny
- teacup
- another person

1. Put a spoon into a glass of water. Look at the glass from the side. Why do you think the spoon appears to be broken?

2. Place a penny on the bottom of an empty teacup. Slowly lower your head down the side of the cup until the penny disappears. Ask someone to slowly pour water into the cup. Why do you think the penny becomes visible when water is added?

Can you explain why a spoon in a glass of water appears to bend?

Experiment 8: What Happens When Light Passes from Air to Water or Glass?

Things You Will Need:

- experimental set-up from Figure 8b
- water
- rectangular plastic tray
- clear plastic block
- glass or plastic prism
- sunlight

1. Set up the experiment as you did for Experiment 6 (Figure 8b). This time, instead of a mirror, you need a rectangular plastic tray.

2. Nearly fill the tray with water. Being careful not to spill, put the tray of water on the light ray. Turn the tray so that the light strikes the tray of water at an angle. What happens when the light ray passes from air into water? Is any of the light reflected? Does the light bend when the light ray is perpendicular to the water tray?

3. Remove the tray and place a clear plastic block on the light ray. Again, turn the block so that the ray strikes the block at an angle. What happens when light passes from air into clear plastic? Does it happen when the light ray is perpendicular to the plastic?

4. Remove the plastic block. Place a glass or plastic prism on the light ray so that it strikes the prism at an angle. Does the light bend? If you bend the light more and more what happens to the light coming out of the prism?

5. Take the prism outdoors. Can you bend sunlight to produce a spectrum (rainbow of colors)? Use a hose to spray water so that sunlight can be reflected back to you. Can you see a rainbow?

Refraction in Nature

Nature is a wonderful source of refraction! One example is a mirage. You can often find a mirage while riding in your car on a hot sunny day. Going up a long, straight incline you may see what looks like a lake at the top of the hill. Of course, there is no lake on the road! What you see is light from the blue sky refracted (bent) by the hot air above the road. Too bad . . . a swim might have been nice.

A mirage in the desert of Africa makes it look as though water is up ahead. It is just an illusion.

As you have found, light is refracted when it goes from one substance to another. Hot air is not the same as cooler air. From the point of view of light, hot air is a different substance than cooler air. The light refracts when it passes through air at different temperatures.

The sun also plays tricks! It is not where it appears to be when rising and setting. The sun can actually be seen when it is *below* the horizon! Figure 10 shows you why this is true. Sunlight passing through layers of Earth's atmosphere is refracted and bent downward. As a result, it appears to be higher than it is in reality.

Look and listen while out in the world for examples of refraction. For sound, as well as light, can be bent.

Refraction: An Explanation

When part of the spoon enters the water it will appear to be broken or bent. Light coming from the part of the spoon under water is bent as it enters air. However, light from the part of the spoon out of water is not bent.

At first, after you lower your head, light from the penny in the teacup can't reach your eyes. Adding water allows light leaving the water to bend downward as it enters air. The refracted light is bent enough so that you can now see the penny.

When light passes from air into water or clear plastic it is bent. Some of the light is also reflected. The light does not bend when the light ray is perpendicular to the water or plastic.

Either kind of prism can bend the light ray if it strikes the prism at an angle. If the light is bent enough, it breaks into colors (a spectrum). Outside, the prism can produce a spectrum using sunlight.

You can use a hose to make a personal rainbow! Light reflected and refracted by the water droplets creates the rainbow of colors. The rainbow you see when it rains and the sun shines is formed the same way. Pretty neat, right?!

Figure 10

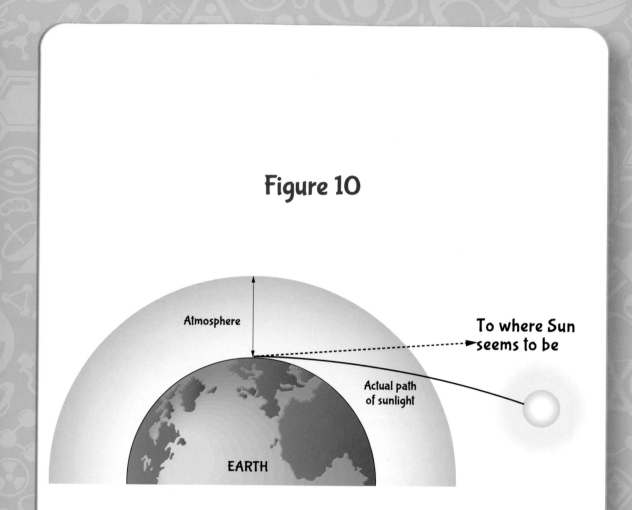

The rising sun is actually below the horizon. The atmosphere refracts the sun's light. This makes the sun appear higher than it really is.

A Lens: Bending Light to Make Images

You have seen how reflected light makes an image in a mirror. How else can we make an image using light? Refraction is all around us but can it help us make an image? Let's find out.

Experiment 9: A Convex Lens

Things You Will Need:

- convex lens
- window opposite a light-colored wall
- bright outdoor scene

A convex lens is the kind found in a camera or magnifying glass. It is thick in the middle and thinner around the edges.

1. Find a window opposite a light-colored wall. A bright scene should be visible through the window.

2. Hold a convex lens near the wall and move it back and forth until you see an image of the outside scene on the wall. What do you notice about the image? What does that mean is happening to the light rays as they pass through the lens? Does the image remind you of a pinhole image?

Unlike the mirror images you have seen, these images are real. This is because light rays coming from all points on an object are brought together. They come together at corresponding points on the image created through the convex lens. Why are pinhole images real images?

A magnifying glass is a convex lens. Use one to project an image of a distant scene onto your wall.

A Lens and Images: An Explanation

The image created through the convex lens was upside down or inverted. The rays from the top of the scene were on the bottom of the image and the rays from the bottom of the scene were on the top!

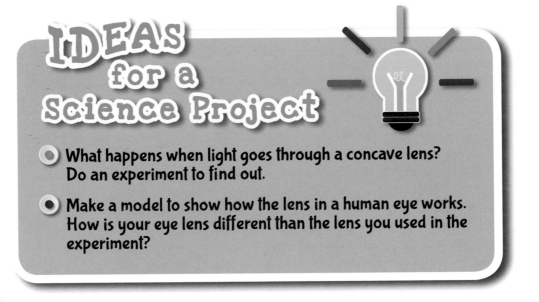

IDEAs for a Science Project

- What happens when light goes through a concave lens? Do an experiment to find out.

- Make a model to show how the lens in a human eye works. How is your eye lens different than the lens you used in the experiment?

Spreading Light (Diffraction)

Because you are now a virtual light expert you know light generally travels in straight lines. You also know it will often bend when passing from one substance to another. However, there are other ways to change light's standard path. Let's see what happens to light when it passes through a narrow opening or along the edges of objects.

Experiment 10: Light Through a Narrow Slit

Things You Will Need:

- clear tubular bulb with one long vertical filament like the one you used in Experiment 2
- two tongue depressors or coffee stirrers
- tubular fluorescent light bulb

When light goes through one or more narrow slits it stops traveling in a straight line and spreads out.

1. Turn on the clear tubular light bulb with the long vertical filament. Look at the filament through two of your fingers held very close together. Your fingers should make a narrow vertical slit. What do you notice about the light that comes trough the slit?

2. You may be able to see the effect even better with two tongue depressors or coffee stirrers. Hold the depressors or stirrers very close together. Look at the light filament through the narrow slit made by the depressors. Hold the slit close to your eye. What do you see? Can you see any colors?

3. Repeat the experiment by looking at a tubular fluorescent light. Do you see the same bright and dark bands? Do you see colors?

   The spreading of light as it passes through a narrow slit or hole is called diffraction. Diffraction can be explained if we assume that light behaves like waves.

   Look at the water waves in the photograph on the next page. See how they spread out when they pass through a narrow opening.

Notice how the waves of water spread out after passing through a narrow opening.

Spreading Light (Diffraction): An Explanation

To explain diffraction, we can think of light as behaving like water waves. When water waves go through a narrow opening they spread out. Light does the same thing on a smaller scale!

From dawn until dusk, you live in a world filled with light. Now you know a great deal more about how that light behaves. We hope you enjoyed these experiments. You can learn more about the world around you by taking a look at the other books in this series, which investigate color, sound, animals, stars, and time. Keep exploring, scientist!

GLOSSARY

convex lens—A lens that causes a beam of light passing through it to come to a point or into focus.

diffraction—When light passes a sharp edge or narrow slit and rays are deflected to create fringes of light and dark spots.

images—Likenesses of objects created by reflecting or refracting light, such as what you see in a mirror or camera.

inverted—When the top and the bottom of something are reversed.

mirage—An optical illusion caused when light is refracted by hot air.

perpendicular—A line is perpendicular to another if it meets or crosses at a 90-degree (or right) angle. The letter L forms a right angle.

reflection—An image of something being thrown back from a mirror or other reflective surface.

refraction—The change in direction of a light ray when it passes from one substance to another.

LEARN MORE

Books

Berne, Jennifer, and Vladimir Radunsky. *On a Beam of Light: A Story of Albert Einstein.* San Francisco: Chronicle Books, 2013.

Johnson, Robin. *What Are Light Waves?* New York: Crabtree Publishing Co., 2014.

Navarro, Paula, and Anjels Jimenez. *Magical Experiments with Light and Color.* Hauppauge, NY: Barron's Educational Series, 2014.

Websites

Ducksters

ducksters.com/science/light.php

An educational website with physics experiments for kids.

Science Kids

sciencekids.co.nz/light.html

Learn more about light with these fun science and technology experiments.

INDEX